Nothing Vs. Everything Vice Versa

Keith Barbour

DEDICATION

To my family and all love ones. Don't be afraid to break the barriers.

CONTENTS

ACKNOWLEDGMENTS

I would love to acknowledge all my family members from the Payne, Moore, and Barbour family. I am indebted to you all. My family is the main reason for this confidence. Who in they right mind would write about nothing vs something? Only me!

I would also like to mention my friends. You guys all give me the strength to keep fighting. All my brothers are sisters are out here making a name for themselves. It is so good to see. I'm very indebted to you all also.

1 MEANING OF WORDS

You know what irritates my soul? The fact that there is so much power wasted into the bottomless pit of one's ego. Many individuals live to please life itself. Life is a state of being and an entity at the same time. What are words and how can they change my life? Words are entities too. We cruise through life wondering our power and worth in this huge circle of a planet with an unbearable gravitational pull. Many who dare to leave the planets they pull find out many truths. The truth is that we give power to words making them come alive. Our deepest fears and dreams manifest through the night into the morning without us knowing. Words, words, and words. Everything, the little things we say, can change life within a space block of holes milliseconds. Nothing we do is a coincidence.

Words can change moods and the perspectives of someone's life. It is actually crazy to realize the significance of the frequency that leaves our mouths to create small little pockets of this world we call home. Understanding this power comes at a cost. You then learn the reasons for what's been lost. Make sure you understand the power of your words and be precise. Understand that the words you say can create new worlds and opportunities; therefore, the more positive approach creates the best chance for success.

2 NOTHING

Nothingness is a state of being.

Bothering me during my peace puts my soul

in a state of feeling.

Wait, can souls even feel?

Why can't I just chill?

Why do we always have to stay for the

thrill?

I don't want just some love.

It would be nice to understand the reason

I'm enough.

Black holes in space can't change the pace.

Of what? The race to the end my friend.

Is the end really nothing?

Please, it has to be something.

What is the reason for everything I just said?

Nothing…….

Be honest.

That is when your soul is calmest.

Feeling black pits.

Death trying to come into the mix

Don't run away from it.

How far can we really get?

You ask for help.

No response, then you melt.

You scream.

Should you be worried?

Should you live in a hurry?

No.

Nothing is peace. Relax…

To be nothing is the situation everyone goes

through.

Billions don't know me and billions don't

know you.

Why is that such a bad thing?

What are you not grasping?

Do you want to be something so bad?

If so, maybe I'm Glad.

We all will be nothing 1 day.

Just not today.

Nothing matters until you make it matter...

You exist because nothing exists

So, take it or leave it.

Drop it or receive it.

Miss it or forget it.

Understand its importance.

Undermine its dormancy.

Nothing comes for all.

Without nothing we 'd be nothing at all.

Something has to exist for nothing to exist.

3 Everything

Having it all can be a blessing or a curse

Putting all before all can have you doomed

to the worst?

Being patient is hard when you want the

whole bunch

It leaves your soul bundled in a crunch

Please just believe that having it all will

either benefit or destroy you

Be careful of your emotions before the devil

employs you

Angels from afar tell you to be content

But the television shows leave you without

sense

Pollution of the mind can be brought even

with majority

Learning to not need all comes with

maturity

Blind your ambitions for a second and be

thankful for it all

Many people shall rise, but their prior

dreams could fall.

Your purpose isn't written it stone to be

changed

Accept everything for nothing in exchange

4 I WANT NOTHING

There is power in understanding the power
of nothing. In this case, a thing represents
the quietness of one's goals, work-life,
ideas, and more. There is a time and place
for everything. I believe everything needs a
quiet mode or rest period. Rest periods could
be manifesting during meditation, sleep, not
talking during the day, or anything else that
doesn't use much energy. All the energy
bottled up during the rest period will be
utilized accordingly.

5 I WANT EVERYTHING

Our greedy flesh has funneled our
minds with the idea of abundance. We want
anything shiny, green, yellow, blue, rich,
extravagant, but will sacrifice anything to
get it. Even our moral compass. Is having
anything you want really that special? Is that
the purpose of humanity? If every human
had everything, then who would appreciate
having nothing? Everything would be
stagnant and people would not worry.
Having everything can be dangerous. You
begin to want more and more. This creates a
chaotic mindset clustered in everyone else's

business. After you receive the list of wants,

then you impede other's needs. It's an

endless cycle of jealously and hate. Be

grateful for what you have as an individual.

6 BALANCE

Balance is free
Balance is key
Balance is you
Balance is me

Nothing will decrease
Everything won't cease
Nothing will fade
Everything will increase

Understand that balance is needed

Patience in your situation is needed

Love for yourself is needed

Love for others are needed

Understand others

Forgive others

Forgive yourself

Understand yourself

Be Balance

7 PURPOSE

We all need a purpose. There needs to be a reason for every action and emotion in all aspects of life. Your journey will consist of many things, but your purpose is the key to preservation and domination. This message applies to all. It doesn't matter if you grew up in a rich or poor household. The only thing that separates the two is time. Some people need extra time to relax, while others have to use it sparingly. Regardless, purpose doesn't look for backgrounds or riches. It seeks a person who is determined to defy all odds. Always remember it's

where you start, not finish.

8 CONCLUDING POEM

There is so much beauty in life

                No need to be upset

You can blink twice

                And have nothing left

Appreciate every memory that you can

borrow to hold

       Be patient with your dreams because you

           never know what the future holds

About the Author

Keith Barbour is a former division 1 athlete that has control of his destiny by putting his time in efforts into multiple businesses. He owns a clothing brand, produces music, and more. Keith is a work horse and he is determined to build an amazing legacy. His reasoning for this stem back to the place where it all began. His childhood. Keith grew up having to take on the adult role at an early age. Sadly, his grandmother suffered from dementia after the passing of his grandfather. His family had no choice, but to take her in and take care of her needs.

So, while the other kids were outside playing, Keith had to stay in with his grandmother. When times get hard, he understood that things could always be worse. His family struggled trying to find ways to pay for her hospital bills. It took a tax on everyone. So, he vowed to never be put in this position again. Never. You could stare into his eyes and see a look that was inhuman. You could say it created a monster. Nobody knows what he feels or thinks, but they know he's special.

Made in the USA
Middletown, DE
07 January 2023

21634264R00015